LAYERS

POETRY BY

ARTHUR SMITH II

ISBN: 978-1-953760-11-1

Printed in the United States of America

Pure Thoughts Publishing LLC

www.PureThoughtsPublishing.com

LAYERS

Poetry by:
Arthur Smith II

This book has been a long time coming. I want to thank my family and friends that have encouraged me along the way. You've held me accountable to my gift. You have supported and inspired me far more than I could ever express. For all the times I said, "Read this!" and you did, thank you!

To my Queen,

You've stood by my side through some unbelievable times. People would look at us in amazement if they knew our story. Thank you for your support and encouragement! You're my number one fan, and I'll always love you for that and so much more.

To my kids,

Daddy loves you more than you could ever truly know. Still, it is your love that keeps me going. It's your love that makes me get up when I want to stay down. It is the greatest honor to be your father. I will always work to be the best possible example of what a man looks like. If I could protect you from every hurt in life that you will experience, I would. But knowing that I can't, I need you to know that I will always be with you during those times of growth. Thank you for all the love and laughs!

To the visionaries, to the avenue creators, to those who give a platform to people like me, you are appreciated. Thank you for following your heart. In doing what you were created to do, others are afforded the opportunity to become who they are created to be. Thank you to everyone that has ever written with me. Thank you to those who have inspired my pen through the usage of your pen. You all being great has stretched me to be better. I'm eternally grateful!

To Q,

I love you. I miss you! I know you would be proud, and a huge supporter had I did this sooner.
Forever in my heart!

Lastly, to God

There is no me without You! I asked for this gift at a time that I was losing all my marbles, and You granted my request. This gift has kept me balanced throughout the years. I'm in awe of what You have inspired. Thank you for never taking your hand off me when You were well within your right. I pray that You continue to move my hand to write. Life, love, and healing come through You and what You inspire.

CONTENTS

WRITING

To me, writing is one of the greatest reminders that we are made in God's image. It gives the writer the ability to create worlds, lives, atmospheres, healing, isolated moments that live eternally. Writing permits the writer to explore and create from any perspective desired, and that is necessary. Appropriately titled, Layers, this book represents many different layers of myself. I'm a man that loves. I'm a man aware of my surroundings and the actions of others. I am a man that loves to think and create. I'm a man that is just totally random. In this book, I took the liberty to write from a plethora of perspectives. In this book, I wanted to honor other artists whose work influenced and provoked me to write. In this book, I wanted to share a small piece of my heart. I always tell people that my writings are true to life, but not necessarily true to my life. My hope is that you can find yourself somewhere within one or some of these poems. Thank you for reading – Love you, be Blessed!

LAYERS

Hell On Earth

In the beginning
your words took away darkness
your presence blew away toxins
Finally allowing me to breathe
In the beginning
you created in me a new image
Called it beauty in your eyes
For the first time
I was able to believe
you
Speaking
Allowed the best of me
To be given
Everything inside
Was living
Foundation
Solid
Is what I thought
We were building
Thought I was seeing Heaven
Turns out I wasn't seeing that well

So blinded by an image
I couldn't see the tale
As my Earth begins to swell
To the forthcoming
Of what am I to tell
Together
We made angelic music
But he thought more highly of himself
Became so vainly conceited
That he tripped and fell
We should have been a trinity
But now we're down one third
I love you with all my heart
But hate I listened to his word
In the beginning
I never imagined
You'd be my hell on Earth
In the beginning
I never imagined
Darkness being worse
In the beginning
I never imagined
Toxins could come from you
In the beginning
I never imagined
How wrong of me you'd prove

Make It Home

I awake in the morning

Afraid to walk out the door

There's no telling

What the world has in store

Fall to my knees

Purify myself

Feed my temple

Getting a grip on my mental health

Can't lay down

Facing my fears

Kissing my loves

Hiding my tears

Behind the wheel

I pray

Make clear

My way

Unsure of what actions to take

What words to say

An unnatural smile

I'll check in now

Maneuvering

Calculated steps
Not trying to piss off
Make no one upset
Not too slow
Not too quick
Not too soft
Not to aggressive
But just right
If there is such a thing
Being it's all relative
On another's sight
Day is turning to night
Back behind the wheel
Lord, please don't let me see
Those red and blue lights
I just want to end
Where I began
Resting in arms
As my loves
Find rest
In the arms
They find strength in

I Need To Know It Will Be Okay

A past of no worries

A past of no fear

A past of your presence

But now you're not here

And it's not like I wished you away

You don't know how much I wanted you to stay

Though my wants are irrelevant

And the reality is evident

Your presence

Will not linger on

In my residence

Needing

But not wanting

To move on

And I need to know

It will be okay

To enjoy the day

To love another

The way…

I need to know

It will be okay

To hold a hand
To once again depend
To allow my heart to mend
To never have to pretend
That I'm…
I need to know
It will be okay
I really need to know
It will be okay
That I'm happy
Without you

Roses Are Red

No one has ever said
Why that line
Is so routinely read
How can a rose
Relate to a beauty
That it can't equate
How can it compare to love
Does it provide
Does it willingly make the choice to die
Does it take action
When anything big or small needs to happen
No
It does none of the above
So again
How can it compare to love

Sometimes

Sometimes I desire a kiss
From a set of lips
That is full of meaning
Yet meaningless

Sometimes I want to be held captive
By liberating arms
With no fear of being torn apart
Their caress would cause no harm

Sometimes I want to be loved
Free and clear
The kind of love
That makes the world cheer

Sometimes

Sometimes I desire to cherish the day
No fuss
No drama
Just go and come as I may

Sometimes I want to scream at the top of my lungs
Be the voice of justice
For my people, for my children
Who are constantly done wrong

Sometimes I want to write
Everything my heart wants to recite
Sometimes I just want to write
All day, all night

Sometimes

Should Pen and
Paper Cease to Exist

I'd write in the sand
Though it wouldn't be safe
For at any given time
The ocean will erase

I'd write with a rock
On the concrete
Only to be pissed
When the city cleans the street

Or maybe
I'd write on the tablet of your heart
Only struggle,
Knowing where to start

Surely Not

Wish conversations flowed like the rivers of Jordan
Wish understanding was our state of residence
Wish simplicity was more prominent than complexity
Wish laughter and happiness erupted like volcanos

What makes things so difficult
Why is every step so full of strife
When will tranquility
Be present in life

Is it only us
That fails to operate in harmony
Is it only us
Who dwell in perpetual misery
Is it only us
Surely not
Peace exists
It's really out there
Though we never seem to find it
Is it only us
Surely not

The Night

Inspired by Chrisette Michelle's Get Through the Night

Tough

Decisions have to be made

Even if they go against dreams of the day

I love you

I really do

But

I love me

A lot more than equal

And as much

As much

As I want

Us

If you don't

We

Won't

And it's tough

Your touch

Has become part

Of my regimen

I crave it

Day to night

Beginning to end

Still

Tonight

Tears run

Moon dims

No sun

For joy

For joy

Comes in the morning

My greatest yearning

Is a torturous burning

No matter how hard I grip

You're already out of my grasp

So to what am I holding

Seems like I'm the last to ask

And it's tough

Finally facing the reality

That has always been in plain sight

You're not my knight

And as much as it hurts, baby

That's alright

Because as the rise of the sun

Is imitated by open palms

Letting go of the harm

Finally able to move on

And oh, how I can't wait

But first

First

I must

Get through the night

Ponderings

I remember life
I remember smiles
I remember happy
But haven't seen it in awhile

Day by day
I die a little inside
It used to be easy to mask
But it now it's impossible to hide

The hurt
Too much to bear
And I want to scream out
This **** ain't fair

How can purity
Be so defiled
How can love
Be so vile

Attempting to shake off

The disdain
Of the life
I maintain

Trying to rebuild
But how do I refrain
From doing the same
To another

How do I get close
And not pollute
How do I confess love
Without being their ugly truth

Compel Me

Compel me
To want to write libraries
About the love shared
Between us two

Compel me
To want to solve the mysteries
Understanding what on earth
Draws me to you

Compel me
To not even bother to solve
For some knowledge
Is not meant for me at all

Compel me
To seek your skin
For when you're away
I go through withdraws

Compel me

To lay down my life
For yours

Compel me
To serve you
And not think it's a chore

Compel me
To know that you are
To understand that I am
And together we can

Kiss of Betrayal

Sacred
Meant for two
A pure form of intimacy
Thought to be
Between me and you

Let's Tell the Truth

Let's tell the truth
We all talk about stopping the violence
But never act on it

Let's tell the truth
Until it hits close to home
There is no move with the meant

Let's tell the truth
When it hits home
We want the world to stop
Addressing how we've been wronged

Let's tell the truth
We all play a part in this thing
So we can stop shifting the blame
It's easy to look back
On the lack
Of action from past generations
But what are you
What am I

What are we doing
In this generation
What are we teaching
What are we displaying
What are we learning
How are we applying wisdom
Who are we reaching out to
Do we patrol our blocks
Are we creating means
To eradicate idleness
What do we demand of those coming up
Are we lifting our hands and giving up
Who washed their hands of us

Let's tell the truth
Many died
For us to live
But no one died
For us to live like this
We don't read
We don't stand up boldly in or for unity
We kill our brother
Deal death to one another
Then want to erupt
When a cop kills one of us
How dare we

Let's tell the truth
We want the preacher to lie
Speaking good over a missing life
"We'll see them again by and by
When Jesus cracks open that sky
Mama, Daddy, you will reunite
So please baby, please don't cry"

Let's tell the truth
They didn't live in peace
So how can they rest in it

Let's tell the truth
They lived by the bullet
And karma is a gun

Let's
Tell
The truth
Lynching will cease
When we stop tying the noose
When we take off our hood of ignorance
And put on the cloak of intellect
Only when we understand the pride of self
Will we overcome

The oppressions of the rest

We are kings and queens

Teach it to your self

You're not worthless

You have a price

That others can't afford

We are kings and queens

Model it to your offspring

Our walk should say

You

Are

Greater

Greater than the death that surrounds

You

Are

Greater

Greater than the education deemed suitable for

You

Are

Greater

Greater than the prison system created to cage

You

Are

Greater

You

Are

Greater

You

Are

Greater

No one should be allowed

And I mean no one

To treat you as less

Not even yourself

How Dreams Are Made

Flesh to flesh

Unashamed

This moment is the best

Let me explain

Soft kisses

Placed on shoulder blades

Hands run gently over spine

This is how dreams are made

The absence of time

Uncertainty

Torn

Mixed emotions

Passion with hatred

Desire with repulse

Needing acceptance while completely rejected

Longing to be touched, but skin crawls

Loving who loves her back

Incomplete

With complete might

To move on

She tries

Still at night

Her heart cries

He loves me enough to die

But not to be by my side

How does one receive so much

While being given so little

How can one pledge death

Without time

Knowing the possibilities

And realities

She burns with excitement

Drawn like a painter

To a canvas

She craves to be in his arms

Already in his grasps

For a time that will never pass

Knowing that if…

(Pleasant sigh)

It would last

If…

One of the smallest words ever created

Yet, it brings the highest level of uncertainty

She

Tormented and pleasured

By the thought

Today, Forever, Yesterday

Today

I sit in an extended gaze

Contemplating forever

And all its possibilities

Awakened by misery

Because choices of yesterday

Have made all possibilities

Fade away

Equal

They say all men are created equal
Though they all are not given equal portions
They all are not given equal opportunities
They all are not given equal resources
But created equal nonetheless
While being held to the "SAME" standards

The say all men are created equal
Though only some can wear hoods
Through hoods
And never be misunderstood
But created equal nonetheless

They say all men are created equal
But only some are killed for sport
As if they have no worth
And the remainder is penalized
For falling victim to the un-(IN)-tentional divide
But created equal nonetheless
No matter how long we've been looking for the evidence

They say all men are created equal

While many look for the sign

Though with the current state of affairs

It appears we've gone back in time

With modern day lynching

By police reprimanded with paid suspensions

They need to see a response

But we don't want your family to lack

Oh, them

It's not our concern that daddy, uncle, and brother never comes back

But created equal nonetheless

They say

A New Song

I'm your favorite song
On a dynamic album
That you never fully hear
Sing the same words
Over and over and over
Because it's soothing to your ears
Lyrics meet you where you are
Begetting a smile
No longer do you feel alone
Comfortable with consistent hurt
Too wounded to see
That life does in fact go on
If you simply move to the next song
But you have me stuck in a groove
Singing the same sad tunes
Warped from the abuse
Though there is much more
That I have in store for
You
Don't have to move
No

Let me

Transition

Usher you into the presence

Of a renewed state

Introduce you to a new song

That has a slightly different pace

Your perspective

It gives a slightly different take

Allowing you to break

Free

Of aching's consistency

Of misery

Attempting to overtake your future's history

Bringing you back to a past

Before you knew that gift

Would become an unwanted present

You

Don't have to move

No

Let me

Transition

Usher you into a time

When cares were delightful

When the biggest concern is

How do I show my freedom

Do I run

Do I dance

Do I sing

Do I take another by the hand

Bleed

I needed you to bleed
I needed you to bleed
I needed you to bleed
For no other reason
Than for me to see you bleed

I See You

I see you

Even when you try to hide

I see you

And the tears you won't let fall from your eyes

I see you

Your smile as a guise

Jealous

Clear blue skies
Chilled waves to match
Light brown sand
Caressing your feet and hands

Jealous is my stance

She Wants To Be Loved

She wants to be loved
Nothing more
Nothing less
Simply loved
Nothing complex
But getting beyond complexity
In a place full of embrace
Has proven to be a challenge for
Her presence
No one faced
Every twitching arm
Compels her to leap for joy
Then crash in sorrow
For her actions
Aren't equally followed

She wants to be loved
Nothing more
Nothing less
Simply loved
Nothing complicated
Just understand

She's been hurt
Slightly jaded
Though still capable of
Giving perpetually
Of herself
Knowing her worth
Despite the neglect
Searching for one
To gift her respect

She wants to be loved
Nothing more
Nothing less
Simply loved
Nothing difficult
Longing to be held
Sincerely
Chest to chest
To fall in the arms of another
To feel safe and secure
Knowing that her insecurities
Will not be ridiculed
Longing to breathe in
The life that she exhales
All while
Building truth
On the Rock that prevails

Progression

Soft kisses

Gentle touch

Strong passion

I Follow

I never saw the trail you blazed
But somehow
It was encoded in my DNA
Embedded in my mental GPS
As subconsciously
I follow every step

An Honest Take

I wonder what people see
When they look into my eyes
If they are in fact
Windows to the soul
Then it's a must
I put up blinds with no holes
For if people saw
They wouldn't be able to hold
This truth…

By nature
I am a protector
Oft
That means
Protecting others
From me
Not saying that I am harmful
But the things I hold inside…

These thoughts…
My soul…

The cry of my heart…

Masking

Has become an Art

Carefully

Strategically

Covering over hurt

With painted smiles

Brushed on happiness

Stroking

Daily

While dying the same

For betraying truth

For displaying

A made-up face

A falsified life

In all my honesty

I've become a liar

Don't put me on the stand

No longer a credible witness

Perjury is all I can…

A clown

Mandated smiles

Despite the frown

Resurrection desired

For a spirit residing

Six feet under ground

"Lazarus, come forth!"

My soul longs to hear

Though, it's been quite some time

And these words have not graced my ears

Ye though my soul

Resides in the Valley of the Shadow of Death

My being still hopes

To breathe a joyful breath

To experience happiness

With every step

Showing true self

Learning the Art of freedom

With an honest take

On being blessed

The Duality of Distance

When believing
The say of they
Absence makes the heart grow fonder
Through being away
They say
Our love holds stronger

Still

Distance creates a void
An opportunity
For others to be enjoyed

Spiderman

Let's play a game of what if
What if
Spiderman's real strength
The true source of his powers
Came from the undying love
Of what he could never have
What if
His true strength
Came from the complete sacrifice
Of his heart's desire
What if
What if you were Spiderman
How much strength
Would you have

Hands

How do hands intended to heal

Cause so much hurt

How do hands design to produce pleasure

Generate so much pain

If I Must

Allow me to reintroduce myself

My name is Art

Birth name Arthur

Some call me son

Others call me brother

One calls me husband

Two call me daddy

These are the things that make me happy

Some want to call me boy

Some will call me, "Nigger"

Some will call me a "Big Bad Dude"

Others will have itchy trigger fingers

These are the things that scares me

I have two babies

That need their dad

It brings tears to my eyes

Making me sad mad

That on any given night

A murderer can hide behind a badge

But I don't fear death

I fear becoming a senseless hashtag

More than willing to give my life

So my babies aren't forced

To live in a world

Where they can be gunned down for

A stalled car

While leaving school

For wanting to return home

After leaving a job interview

For playing freely in a park

For having a childish moment in Walmart

For having their hands in the air

On their feet or back

To Protect and Serve doesn't even care

For one being on one's own property

Wanting to protect their home

For exercising their "Rights"

And still reaping physical harm

So

If I must die

Let it not be in vain

I'm not looking to be made famous

I have no need

For Fox News to know my name

I'm just a man

Who wants his kids to be seen as human

I'm just a man

Who wants his babies
To grow up in a world
That loves its neighbor
As himself
I'm just a man
Who wants his lineage
To have a chance
If I must die
I will die with dignity
If that means my babies
Will live in liberty

Visions

Inspired by Stevie Wonder

We spend all day
Talking
Laughing
Asking questions
About nothing
And somehow
Our nothings
Always seem so relevant
Gaining knowledge of no meanings
That's o'so meaningful
The visions of our minds
Create a world
Apart from any
That has ever been seen
But what I'd like to know
Is how our visions can be so serene
And our reality
Such a lonely scene
As if you weren't meant for me
And I for you

As if you and I weren't meant

To bring forth little royal beings

As if our paths intertwining

Wouldn't bring relief

From what seems

A lifetime worth of lying

We spend all day

Though I'm tired of the waste

It's beyond evident

That we are meant to be mates

So what I'd like to know

Is if you're willing to accept fate

If you are willing to

While allowing me to

Be

All that the other needs

What I'd like to know is

Why do we spend all day

Talking

Wondering about a lifetime

When we should be living it

What I'd like to know is

If someday soon

You'd be willing

To pledge the love of we

Making a true vision of reality

To exist

Noise

She listened to noise
Until she was introduced to music
At times she still
Gravitates towards noise
For it shaped her past
But music
Has a hold of her future
And won't let her go

She listened to noise
Until she was introduced to lyrics
Now with the noise
She's a much sharper critic
No longer easily moved
With random mumbles
For it's the sincere and honest
That promotes her growth

View

Through damaged lens
Seeing nothing that you want
Though everything you need
Is ever before
You
View
Through damaged lens

Code

I feel the need to speak in code

And those

Who understand

Will understand

And those

Who don't

Will

With the fulfillment

Of the plan

You Can't Tell Me

You can't tell me
What
How
When
Where
To feel
You can't tell me
That none of this is real
And still you'll try
So I guess
I'm supposed to be blind to the fact
That
Some prey for game
Though I'd be crucified
If I did the same
So I guess
I'm supposed to turn the other cheek
When so many are hurt by a sheet
You can't tell me to forget
Because it happened so long ago
No

It happened last year

Last month

Last week

Yesterday

You can't tell me to forget

The irony

Even if I did attempt

It would be brought back to my remembrance

When actions of yesterday

Are repeated today

You can't tell me not to cry

While seeking justice

When the ones who are supposed to serve it

Rob so many of it

You can't tell me

Not to prepare my son

For potential dangers he may face

Because the hue of his skin

So many hate

You can't tell me

Not to teach my daughter

You're far more than erotic

More than a fantasy for use

You are a beautiful spirit

With an abundance to contribute

You can't tell me

You don't see color

As a harmless attempt

To excuse away my blackness

You can't tell me

You can see the difference between him and her

While refusing to acknowledge

The differences between you and me

And yes

I know there will be many that refute

Many that disagree

Though disagreement

Doesn't change reality

Truth

Just because the hatred doesn't come from you

Doesn't mean that hatred doesn't come

You would never walk in my shoes

And I wouldn't advise you to

Because it hurts

That still to this day

All men

Isn't meant for me

Or my daughter

Or my son

Or my wife

Or my mother

Or my sister

Or my brother
Or my father
But I work
And pray
That someday
All men
Will include
All humans

My Soul

My soul
Longs
For
My soul
Yearns
For
My soul
Pleads
For
More
Though I know
Not
How to obtain
As I remain
On my knees
In fervent
Fill me up
Permit my cup
To flow
Over
With
And from
You

Happy

Inspired by Labrinth's Jealous

When I told you
I only want you to be happy
Never was it intended
That you would be happy
Without me
And that's not an arrogant statement
My honest perception
We were meant to be

Without you
I've been overcome
Overcome with a severe case of
I don't…
I won't…
I can't…
I just can't …
Without…

And I see you
With a smile

Greater than the one
That was experienced with me
As it rips my heart in two
To unselfishly be
For thee

When I told you
I only want you to be happy
Never once
Did I perceive
This reality

A Silent Invitation

Lips don't have to part

To know my heart

Eyes don't have to blink

For you to know what I think

Broken Smile

She smiles the smile of a broken soul

26 feeling three times as old

Trapped in a marriage

Where excitement is owed

Pretending

Ending

Happiness

Is no longer shown

In

Living

Misery

Willing to speak

Not

Desiring closeness

Apart from his presence

She

Seeks

Peace

Eludes her

Me

You see me
Though not for who I was
But for who I am
And who I am to be

Honest Aberration

I'm not okay

So often I need tears to flow

But I don't/can't let them

Though they build/swell

As my ducts become damaged dams

Fluids randomly seeping through cracks

Unmasking my

…Super…

Human

Is all that I've ever been

And humans are fragile

Humans bend, crack, and break…

I'm at my point

Standing with all my might

And my knees are buckling

But you blinked

And couldn't see it

As I wear a smile

Masking the weary

Prolonging the faint

The kryptonite works

Satan is succeeding

Steal, Kill, and Destroy

As I wait on life

As dams weaken

Prompting a greater leakage

Praying no one finds out my secret

I'm miserable

Despite what I've been speaking

Honesty has always been given

Though this is its aberration

Moments of sunshine do exist

These are the expressions

That typically flows from these lips

But these truths are

Deeper…

Darker…

A more in depth perspective of my world

Where nights last for days

Where days last for but a breath

Vulnerable

Because for the weary

There is no rest

Always on guard

Trying to protect me from you

And you from myself

My heart hurts

And hurt people

Hurt people

Attempting to remain to myself

To prevent the sequel

For the pressures of life

Leave me vexed…

Guitar and Drums

There is a place
A special place
A deep
Deep place
Hidden far beyond
Where eyes can seek
A place embedded so deep in my soul
That even I can't reach

This special
Deep
Hidden
Embedded place
Holds something
Capable of moving
The most intimate parts of me
You were there
In that place
Long before I was aware
Strumming my love song
Charting the chords of my delight

Climbing the scale--well to my heart
Your melodic voice sends chills
Vibrating through my being
You are the rhythm
To this nation
The lead
To this army

When enlightenment occurred
And a declaration was declared
It was not your name
That was inserted there
There were outside interests
That had my attention
As attentive ears listened
It was their name
That I mentioned

Initially
We seemed a good pair
But falling in and out of love
Never seemed fair
We developed
Just not at the rate that we should
Or to the level that we could
Trying to force our way to a place

Whose fortified walls
Refuse to break
This was not Jericho
So no matter how much they sang
No matter how hard they banged
They weren't strong enough
To move a string
Tension
Wound tight enough to bust skins
A for better or worse relationship
Leaning more to the latter it tends

A Threat

I'm a threat
Educated or not
Violent or not
On the bottom or on top
I'm a threat
Speaking or speechless
Business or street dress
Rested or restless
I'm a threat
Playing or breaking
Twisting or shaking
Right or mistaking
I'm a threat
Supplying or buying
Telling the truth or lying
Whether I'm living or dying
I'm a threat
Guilty or innocent
Hell or heaven sent
Unskilled or experienced
I'm a threat

What's Peace?

What's peace?

Peace is having my father in my house,

Telling me right from wrong.

What's peace?

Peace is being able to retire my mom,

Repaying her for all the hard work she's done.

What's peace?

Peace is buying a home,

With me proclaiming how I want it to run.

What's peace?

Peace is the fulfillment of your dreams,

Then going back to help someone else do the same thing.

What's peace?

Peace is being able to let my kids play in the park,

Without some stranger persuading them to walk off.

What's peace?

Peace is being able to walk in a store,

Without being stared at by Bob, Sue, or Chung.

What's peace?

Peace is having a sane state of mind,

No matter what circumstance I may face at any point in time.

What's peace?

Peace is coming home to a nice warm hug,

Given with sincerity of heart by the woman I love.

What's peace?

Peace is knowing God loves me,

In spite all my misbehavior.

What's peace?

Peace is not about the Middle East,

It's how you feel inside.

What's peace?

Peace is a beautiful thing,

That most never seem to find.

Growth

I'm happy
Without your permission
And it feels good
To be standing here admitting
That I now know
In asking
I was tripping
You didn't make me
The absence of your presence
Didn't break me
In fact it saved me
I've learned
There is no point of wasting time
With a waste of time
Learning to appreciate the value of mine
Once
I gave you a power
That I now revoke
With hindsight being 20/20
I understand that you were a joke

Plea

This is not a poem

It's a plea

I'm tired of seeing us die

Rise

Day in

Day out

You see hashtag (insert name here)

You see injustice

Caused by a broken system

That was "Created" to provide it

You become enraged

Seeing the list grow daily

Thinking

Surely a change is going to come

Surely they will see the errors of their ways

Surely...

Overtaken by tears

Until you're just over tears

These senseless acts consume you

Causing you to want to act

But you don't know how

Being an activist

Makes the target on your back

Even bigger

And I have kids

I don't want to be

A hidden figure

What do you do when it becomes too much

What do you do when cries for help

Go unheard

When you try to point out what's wrong

But it's flipped to make it seem as

Something's wrong with you

When you're told you're ungrateful

You should just be happy you're here

I

Personally

Tried to purge myself of social interactions

Seeing it on my timeline

Time and time again

It became too much

My anger grew everyday

Probably more from feeling helpless in every way

I have to live in this cold

Not meant for me world

My wife and kids have to do the same

Surely a change...

Surely...

But I don't see it coming

Because anyone who tries

Dies

Anyone just trying to get by

Dies

Still

A reckoning is coming

On a side

Everyone will have to decide

We the people are either going to fold

Or be like our lineage

And rise

Magician

You gave the illusion

That we'd remain closer

Than scalp and hair

Teach me how I can just walk away

Teach me how you could just not care

Teach me how to connect without actually connecting

Teach me

Teach me how to be here today

And gone tomorrow

All while forgetting yesterday

Teach me

Go ahead

Be Sensei

I'll be the pupil

Taking in every lesson

Holding dear as if it were a blessing

Teach me how to not give a …!

Please teach me

Teach me how to remove

Every aspect of you

Out of my heart

Teach me how to hurt without hurting

Come on you insensitive bastard

Teach me to be just like you

Why aren't you talking

Is this the magician's creed

You keep the secrets to yourself

While performing these wonders

Legacy Pt. 1

It was da happiest day of my life

I'z married da man of my dreams

I'z married a man

Who would do

Absolutely anything for me

We jumped da broom

For all da world to see

We danced

We sang

It was a celebration for all to enjoy

It was da happiest day of my life

As the celebration turned a bit more personal

There'za knock at da door

He opened to massa saying

"I have a guest in town

And I told him I have the perfect little whore"

He tried shutting the door

Crying out

"My wife is no one's little whore"

He say

"Boy open up, for I'z puts ya through the floor"

"Massa, it's ours wedding day"

He pulled his gun

And there was nothing left to say

I'z watched da man of my dreams

Lose his manhood

As I'z followed behind massa

Da happiest day of my life

In an instant changed

To an even worse eternity

I'z looked back at a newly broken man

Barely able to stands to his feet

Massa say,

"Hurry up

We can't keep him waiting"

I'z walked silently

Preparing for this degrading

We gets to da suite

Dis walk of shame

Transformed me from a bride to a piece of meat

Dis morning was the first time I felt human

Dis evening is teaching me much different

He looked at me with disgusting eyes

He touched me with filthy hands

He had his way with me

And threw me out like the garbage I'z am

He ain't even give me time

To puts on my clothes

Naked

Ashamed

A broken vessel

Trying to pick up the pieces

Of my existence

Back to da place

Where dis nightmare began

Door still open

Man of my dreams still broken

Neither can look da other in da eyes

Da happiest day of my life

Became da night our legacy died

No words

No love resembling motions

Zombies

Though I knows I'z not dead

Because life

From an unwanted source

Grows inside me

Days fade

With not much to say

Unclear

Somehow

I'z love'z and hate'z

What's to come

And unto us

An (un)wanted child is born

Legacy Pt. 2

It was da happiest day of my life
I'z married da most beautiful woman I'z ever seen
It all felt like a dream
To love
And to be loved
Is da most fascinating thing
I'z didn't have much
But her love was all'z I need
We shared ours happiness with all
Jumping the broom
In front of all the world
We'z partied til day turn night
Da time finally came
When she and I were'z to celebrate right
But there'za knock at da door
I'z opened and massa say
"I have a guest in town
And I told him I have the perfect little whore"
I'z tried shutting the door
Crying out
"My wife is no one's little whore"

He say

"Boy open up, for I'z puts ya through the floor"

"Massa, it's ours wedding day"

He pulled his gun

And there was nothing left to say

She walk pass me

Without uttering a word

A few steps out

She looks back

And failure all'z I heard

How does happiness end so fast

One moment I'z living a dream

And in a blink

All'z I can do is scream

I'z built in strength

Though lives in weakness

A man's job is to protect

How does he cope

When his actions are helpless

It seems an eternity

She's been gone

Can't begin to imagine

Her experience

Don't want to imagine

Her thoughts of me

I'z just wants to kill

But I'z can't tell

If that's directed at them

Or me

Paralyzed

A broken shell of what once was

How do'z I face her

If she walks back through the door

It seems an eternity

Fetal on the floor

Hearing her footsteps

Will she want me anymore

Much to my surprise

She crosses da threshold

Short glances

Mutually shared

No words

I'z couldn't bare

Blank

Void

Empty

As she passes

Seeking purity

Attempting

Failing

To rinse

Filth and tears

Fears and nightmares

Days fade

Figures change

I'z shrink

She grows

Fertilized

From an unwanted source

I'z don't want dis seed to blossom

Likewise

I'z don't want her to endure anymore hurt

Paralyzed

Still unable to fully protect

Days fade

And unto us

An unwanted child is born

Legacy Pt. 3

I was born into a family

Being my mother's child

At home

There was broken love

Born into a world

Where there's no love

It's like hate was conceived at the thought of me

Though I've done nothing but breathe

What scene did I interrupt

What life did I destroy for everyone to hate me so much

My mother's eyes look at me strange

My father never calls me son

Only by my name

And though I've yet to do

I always seem to be the center of blame

Many stare

Many point

Many whisper

Though no one speaks

It's some big secret

That no one cares to share with me

Who am I

Why am I so different

Why are hearts filled with malice

And resentment

Towards me

I remember

I remember two things about my dad

A shadow of a man

He worked hard to provide

There was nothing my mom could ask

That she couldn't have

He worked himself into a grave

For her happiness

To always evade

And then I remember

I was young

We were playing catch

It appeared we were having fun together

For the first time

Then he throws the ball

With what seemed all of his might

I chased

And I chased

But it seemed as if the ball would never stop

It traveled so far

I had to wonder

If he wanted either of us back

When I finally got it in my hands

The shadow was gone

Preparing myself

For the loneliest walk home

I looked at my mom

She had tears in her eyes

I looked for my dad

He said

Good luck trying to find

And there it was

Secrets revealed

I now understood why

His eyes were full of disdain

Completely void of pride

Momma's baby

Massa's maybe

___ Life Matters

If I change it

To my life matters

Would you feel any different

Than you do when I say

Black Lives Matter

Would the sting be removed

If the focus was singular

Versus plural

Would it make you feel more safe

If I focused on I

And not my brother

How much more comfortable can I make you

In my discomfort

All Lives can't Matter

If one is so easily disregarded

Seems Simple

Yet this concept is missed by so many

You Don't Have the
Right to Remain Silent

- Inspired by the words of Pastor Hosea Wilson – Greater Faith
Missionary Baptist Church, Gary, IN

There is a difference

You know

Between a right

And a responsibility

When you come through

What we've come through

You don't have the privilege of rights

No

When you come through

What we've come through

You wear the mantle of responsibility

But what are we responsible for

We are responsible for being educated

And educating

We are responsible for

Raising our village

Through supporting our lineage

We are responsible for

Using our voice

To speak life

To speak love

To uplift

To demand justice

We are responsible for

Fighting for those

Who can't fight for themselves

We are responsible for

Fighting with those

Who fight for us

We can no longer afford

To participate in the deeds

That impede the progression of the struggle

We don't have the right to remain silent

In the wrong doing towards our brothers and sisters

We don't have the right to remain silent

In the oppression of any man woman or child

We don't have the right

To remain silent

When these self-evident truths

Life

Liberty

And the pursuit of happiness

Aren't evident for all

From Me To You

I wanted to take a moment to express my gratitude to you the reader. It means the world to me that you would take time to read my thoughts. Hopefully, you could find yourself somewhere within LAYERS. To show my gratitude, I provided a little bonus, a preview of what's to come. Once again, thank you! – Love you, and be blessed!

Dig Deeper

What moves you
What are you so passionate about
that you'll fight for it
What makes you cry
What in this world
keeps you up at night
Why do you hold back
Why won't you share with the world
Why won't you accept
that people need your words
You say you give your heart
But that's all lies
you only give the surface parts

When will you dig deeper
Why dwell in the shallows
When your truths reside in the depths

What are you afraid of
Being exposed
Because the truth of the matter is

you're the last to realize
you're not as strong as you hold

Why won't you dig deeper
your words being hushed
Can never stop the screams of your eyes
They tell the truth
They will never lie
And still…
Still…
you refuse
To allow your words to
Breakthrough
your disappointments
those are really triumphs
Stop thinking you failed
Once you change your perspective
People will breathe
from the words you exhale
Don't you know
inside you lives
the tree of life
Don't you
What good is a doctor
that never uses his hands to heal
What good is an architect
that never takes time to build

What good is your silence
What good are your bare minimum truths
What good is it being a writer
who refuses to show
a vulnerable you

you need to dig deeper
Because right now
I'm ashamed
I'm tired of dying daily
for you to be mediocre
I'm tired of being used
for you to be subpar at best
When you proposed
you offered a commitment
that you've yet to uphold
I need
No scratch that
I demand
That you dig deeper
And if you won't
Please
Be man enough
to leave me alone

Sincerely,
Your Pen

About Author

Arthur Smith II is a son, brother, friend, husband, and father. Arthur is a lover of all things art related. He fell in love with music at an early age. Drawn to both instrumentation and lyrics, a love for writing developed in his early twenties. Writing became the saving grace to his sanity. Quiet in nature, Arthur finds himself writing the words he should probably speak out loud. The cultivation of his personal style came through penning poetry, music, movies, plays, and short stories. Arthur has amassed a large body of work throughout the years. It's now time to share with the world!

Follow me:
FB: AuthorArthur2
IG: AuthorArthur2
Twitter: AuthorArthur2
Website: www.AuthorArthur2.com

www.ingramcontent.com/pod-product-compliance
Lightning Source LLC
Chambersburg PA
CBHW060630100426
42744CB00008B/1576